# CRAZY CLOUD IKKYŪ

VERSIONS AND INVENTIONS

*by* **Stephen Berg**

ZIG ZAG
**P R E S S**

Cover photograph, *Wall Cloud*, copyright © 2010 Eileen Neff

ISBN 978-0-9890912-2-0
Library of Congress Control Number: 2014937755

Composed in Sabon and Optima fonts
by P. M. Gordon Associates, Inc.

Published by ZIG ZAG PRESS LLC, Philadelphia, Pennsylvania
Distributed by MILLICHAP BOOKS LLC

*For information, contact:*
pmillichap@sbcglobal.net

*For Terry*

# Note

Ikkyū, a 15-century Japanese monk and Zen master, was as eccentric and influential in his poetry as in his interpretation of Zen tradition. In an earlier book, *Crow with No Mouth: Ikkyū*, published by Copper Canyon Press, I offered my own "versions" of Ikkyū's poems. In this new volume, most of the poems are free inventions inspired by those earlier renderings.

In *Crow with No Mouth* I acknowledged the scholars whose work I used as a basis for my versions. A handful of poems in *Crazy Cloud* are versions too, based on scholars' translations— but those sources I cannot remember, and I apologize for any absent acknowledgments or thank-yous to scholars whose work supplied the basis for the versions in this book.

—SB

# 1

who's crying outside my door? ask Kyosie if you don't know
men crazy running after things midnight burns blue outside
    my window


green willow red peony journey's finished today
break my staff over my knee bury it in the July snow


mind so calm dream born into this dream of a world
I'll fade morning dew on a grassblade


for thirty years mere mist mere haze
mist haze sixty years eat Buddha shit die

no wind waves huge who uses this road? all streams converge
but a little chunk of cloud wipes out empty space


words phrases of the masters monk hating monk like spitting
        blood
sword mountain's razor peaks all you know


snow on the ground in the mind is how to do it koan
        completes
itself head shaved somebody writes poems hungry


picking the cutest whore to fuck this old monk sings as
        he does it
inspired by her cunt her kisses not a shred of hellish guilt

meditate write poems you idiots argue about bullshit all day
compassion would have fed the starving monk


knowing you'll die destroys you who can you tell work
    play want
don't want be blind deaf senseless can't stop any of it


mind never flows each instant the same past future moon
trapped among branches the drinker fondles his cup


no subject object mystery no form safe life impossible
subject object fire burning my pine floor

toilet paper sutras koans are like the shit smeared on them
not one thought while I wipe my ass

earth corpse heaven corpse gates barriers gone snow
        somewhere a beggar
stops at my door disappears the moment I see him

this cook's amazing one flavor taste the world two spicy fish
gnaw on the head swallow its eyes suck every bone

subject object koan's beyond me sake dissolves it wind
ruffles the pines and cedars clouds millions of people can't
        believe it

zen people fight over zen poets over poetry snail horns safety
    danger
one knife kills one sword protects that gorgeous woman knows


reckless natural thirty years Ikkyū's zen is these hundred meat
    flavors
sake gruel twig tea in one cup


sitting still not there yet laugh at the Surangama Sutra recite
    step into
a brothel once and it happens


koans stories examples deception arrogance grows
girl in the whorehouse wears gold brocade

clear yesterday stupid today reckless easy acute
dark light trust change shade your eyes look into the farthest
    distance


no end beginning this human mind no innate Buddhahood
Buddha's wild talk was innate your mind's a delusion


nothing but fucking on my mind drives me crazy wild fire
    never
destroys it spring breezes grass again


look zen in sickness years back Pai-chang and his hoe
drunk all night facing hell what about some rice money?

thieves never attack the poor one's money is not the king's this
    virtuous
face the root of disaster millions of silver coins worthless


zen's going downhill mistakes then mistakes now spring wind
    humming even
without sake poverty's elegance October


these assholes marching down the hall hands folded *gassho*
    offering incense
flywhisks clapper wooden chair Ikkyū anguished cuts open
    his stomach


incense stink oh how many masters are enlightened talk
    endlessly about zen
how to attain it pious despicable what stinking incense

today's priests are wooden swords seen in a room look real
     but outside in
sunlight split bamboo not good for fighting or anything


zen students have no sense of the truth red purple and gold
     robes veneer
my sincere words like chewing tin I play my music to
     cows horses


always another barrier behind a barrier rules and examples
     can't get across
exquisite white delicious lychee given to us


money's more powerful than a god my legs like brittle twigs
song of the griefstricken cuckoo's blood spring in my heart

almost went crazy from training so hard nothing's better
than fishermen's songs sunset rain clouds moon night after
    night


thirsty you dream of water cold one dreams about fire
I dream of a girl naked in her bedroom that's who *I* am

## 2

watch the cherry blossoms feel
your life suddenly disappear


think of tomorrow the habit of thinking
of tomorrow gone like tomorrow


I didn't build myself a grass-roofed hut deep
in the mountains nevertheless I hate this world


see that streak of lightning across the sky
you

without two things there's not one
and the inkbrushed landscape is very cool


you're going to die that's all so what
begin again always begin again begin


death life the diver's boat is loaded with
is is not but break through the floor and


nobody's a friend on our way through this life
loneliness is a needle in a seething brain

there is there is people say it all the time
but it isn't this mountain echoes answering back

there isn't there isn't we all think
though the mountains cry out that exact thought

if you need to know how to live in both this
world and the so-called other ask someone merciful sincere

you don't have to say one idiotic thing look the
flowers there fall scatter dust

I have to remind myself like a child
willow green blossom red always a dumb child


tell me why with all this grief this pain
we shouldn't want to become a mote in the sky


the mind that's what they call it my ass!
no such thing enlightened with what?


the cloud climbs without anyone helping it
it doesn't read a book of miserable sutras

go ahead talk say things like "nothing special"
be an asshole nothing to say Ikkyū this rock IKKYŪ


the cherries again pink delicate aroma
fall don't know spring will be back


the mind tell me what's the mind prayer?
the breeze that blows through pines in the ink painting?


write something leave it behind
nobody will ever read it

fucked up I want to be that stone Buddha
over there in the corner of the garden


I'll never die I won't go anywhere I'll be here
like a wall that won't answer one of your stupid questions


I wish I could give you something but look at these hands
emptier than air

## 3

nap on the way back from Leaky Road to never-leaking road
what Zen bullshit windy rain rainy wind


once I was never here nothing nature never knew me
this Ikkyū corpse rotting like a plum


as as is your question is as is my answer is as is
mind is a doorway without a door


if you think time exists think again the
mind before you the mind after you die

sins my ass they don't mean anything like milkweed
on the wind and all my guilt milkweed on the wind


nothing I've done is wrong none of it's real
that's why I do nothing anymore that's wrong


what's evil tell me what have you done that's evil
I ask myself not one stinking illusion no illusion


heard it before all the Zen nuts mouth it breeze moaning
    in pines
in the black ink image is consciousness no it's the breeze and
    no pines

the word Buddha is like a barn loaded with cowshit
you don't need to pray to it to smell it

the most powerful truth is that a lie is Buddha lying to himself
and you each step you take nonsense lies salvation's nowhere

rain hail snow ice are your face after your dead skull crumbles
into a thousand pieces and a child carries them home

if I hear one more word about seeking the Buddha way
I'll puke I love the chaos passion hypocrisy I contain

I'm asking myself where I'm from and it's as if when I touch
    my face
it's nobody from a nameless place with four walls where?

they say it's beautiful but I hate the fact that the cherry
    blossoms
fall and are gone and feel the pain

the saucepan's face shaved whiskers on the pebble
the bamboos in the painting sing

these words less meaningful than a dust mote
and what they say is wrong signed Ikkyū

my house is like a single paper screen roofless
wind misses it rain can't make it wet




clouds up there swirling fleeing gray blue white
it's amazing they can't read a single word




ripples on the unaccumulated water of the undug well
a man without a body hauls water from it




somebody just whispered the word enlightenment into my ear
I threw him down and beat his face to a pulp

sure I guess in our deepest nature we're unborn undying
I've heard those notions those terms they make me yawn


crescent full moon no moon nothing is left
dawn and the crescent moon


another Zen idea: the willow the flower have no color
the willow green the flower red you looking at them


anguish grief that's most of what life is
why not love death why not admire ourselves before we
     were born

if I could kill words in my head I would don't give a shit
what they mean nobody's there to read them anyway


we are responsible to express the fact that flowers know
     nothing
of Zen but bloom in spring drop off scatter become dust and
     nobody asked them to


I helped people I probably even stopped a few from killing
     themselves
but this raging fire called me I can't put out


we're born we die even the great masters
even the cat even the wooden ladle I use for soup

even though I know it's noon I don't know what time is
and see that mountain in the distance don't know what space is

I won't die I won't go anywhere I'll still be right here
when you come to see me ask me anything

it's a fake all of it seems real I know what an idiot I am
death isn't something that happens to me and you

only the man of mercy sincerity
sees you

I'd love to give you a gift that would make you happy
but in my sect we have nothing


it's exquisite to push my face into a slice of melon when I eat it
feel the sweet cold flesh wet almost up to my eyes


because I don't think of my body as my body
everywhere I am is the same


no sound no odor that's the mind
any word you use you stole from somebody else

yes it's an echo off the mountain *There is There is*
but not when I'm standing close to it

they say the whole afterlife thing is like numbers written
     on water
I say it's like a stick shoved up my ass

not one cloud hangs over my heart
no mountain hides the moon

I'm alone and so are you always alone
so lonely when we die

what I do is not what I say
it's shameful


lightning evaporates like dew
this ghost of myself


thinking hard about it—I and other people
no difference our minds each other's


don't worry about it dear dear friend I love you
fool sinner condemned saved like me

www.ingramcontent.com/pod-product-compliance
Lightning Source LLC
Chambersburg PA
CBHW032109040426
42449CB00007B/1234